THEMATIC UNIT

My Home and My Neighborhood

Written by Rachel C. Oetken

Edited by David Cook
Illustrated by Bruce Hedges

Cover Art by Cheri Macoubrie Wilson

Teacher Created Materials, Inc.
6421 Industry Way
Westminster, CA 92683
www.teachercreated.com
©*1999 Teacher Created Materials, Inc.*
Reprinted, 2002
Made in U.S.A.
ISBN 1-57690-469-5

Table of Contents

Introduction

My Home and My Neighborhood has been designed to enable young students to demonstrate an understanding of the geography of their neighborhoods, and in particular, their homes. A wide variety of disciplines has been incorporated into the unit, including science, math, music, language arts, literature, and art.

Activities have been constructed to allow students to develop the attributes of good citizenship and character while learning to work with others in a school setting. For example, activities include "building" a home out of one group of materials, requiring that a group work cooperatively.

In keeping with history and social science national standards, students will also demonstrate an awareness of the past, explaining some of the ways in which the "here and now" are different from the "long ago." Activities along this line include a comparison of homes in early America with American homes today.

Each lesson has a correlating activity to be completed. These activities will solicit verbal expression from students while the teacher assesses their understanding.

A variety of good teaching methods have been included, such as the use of visuals and hands-on/minds-on lesson plans.

Directions for a class book, bulletin board ideas, awards, stationery, home connection activities, and letters home are also included in a management section. This section will allow the busy teacher to effectively create a room environment that fits with the theme, as well as communicate with parents.

This thematic unit has been designed to introduce early childhood students to the world around them, beginning with the familiar: their homes and neighborhoods.

Objectives

1. Students will identify the home as a dwelling place for families, a place of shelter from weather, and a means of protection for valuables.

2. Students will compare and contrast the differences between American homes of the early 1900s and American homes of today.

3. Students will have the opportunity to develop some beginning mapping skills.

4. Students will identify, classify, and compare different materials used to build homes.

5. Students will practice safe-home procedures to better prepare themselves for dangerous situations.

6. Students will be given the opportunity to gain a sense of independence and autonomy by performing various jobs commonly done at home.

7. Students will identify neighborhoods as places where families live and work.

Introduction *(cont.)*

Why Whole Language?

A whole-language approach involves students in using all modes of communication: reading, writing, observing, illustrating, experiencing, and doing. Communication skills are interconnected and integrated into lessons that emphasize language as a whole rather than isolating its parts. The lessons revolve around selected literature. For example, reading is not taught as a subject separate from writing and spelling. A child reads, writes (spelling appropriately at his/her level), speaks, listens, etc., in response to a literature experience introduced by the teacher. In this way, language skills grow naturally, stimulated by involvement and interest in the topic at hand.

Why Thematic Planning?

One very useful tool for implementing an integrated whole-language program is thematic planning. By choosing a theme with correlating literature selections for a unit of study, a teacher can plan activities throughout the day that lead to a cohesive, in-depth study of the topic. Students will learn by practicing and applying their skills in meaningful contexts. Consequently, they will tend to learn and retain more. Both teachers and students will be freed from a day that is broken into unrelated segments of isolated drill and practice.

Why Big Books?

An excellent cooperative whole-language activity is the production of "big books." Groups of students can apply their language skills, content knowledge, and creativity to produce a big book that can become a part of the classroom library to be read and reread. These books make excellent culminating projects for sharing beyond the classroom with parents, librarians, other classes, etc. Big books can be produced in many ways, and this thematic unit includes directions for at least one method you may choose.

Learning Centers

Learning centers are an especially effective method of teaching to reach the different types of intelligence of the early childhood student. Learning centers allow for students to explore materials at their own pace, verbalize solutions to activities, and choose topics that interest them most.

Listed below are several possible learning center ideas. Some adaptations may be necessary to meet the needs of your classroom.

☐ *Book Nook Center:* This center should be stocked with books relating to the home. See suggested Book Nook reading list on page 80.

☐ *Building Center:* This center can be filled with an assortment of materials used to build a home such as play dough, craft sticks, buttons, or any classroom "collection" items as well. Allow students to build their own kinds of homes.

☐ *Activity Center:* This center can be changed regularly to provide students with different file-folder games as well as other activities provided throughout the unit.

☐ *Creative Role Play Center:* Allow students to pretend they are in different rooms of the home, using different household objects such as spoons, bowls, and plastic foods to represent the kitchen; or shoes, hats, and suitcases to represent the closet.

☐ *Listening Center:* Students may use this center to listen to various books on tape or songs about homes. See the bibliography on page 80 for suggestions.

☐ *Art Center:* This center is a great place to complete suggested art projects. Make sure that tables and floors are covered. An old plastic table cloth or shower curtain makes for easy cleanup.

☐ *Storytime Center:* This center gives students a place to sit comfortably as they listen to and discuss the story being read aloud. You may wish to provide a variety of carpet squares or pillows.

In a People House
by Theo Le Sieg

Summary

This classic book has colorful illustrations and rhyming words that are sure to capture the attention of any young student. The characters of a mouse and a bird tour the house discussing the different objects they discover. The book is especially helpful for the student with limited English skills because each word is illustrated with a picture. The book also encourages discussions of all the things that are in a "people house," broadening the students' perceptions.

Suggested Activities

Setting the Stage

1. Send home all necessary letters to inform parents of unit activities.

2. Read the title and author of the book aloud, and ask students what they think the book will be about.

3. To improve students' sorting and classifying skills, bring in several different household items, some from each room at home (ideas: toothpaste, a pillow, a serving spoon, a *TV Guide*, etc.). Ask students which room each item belongs in.

4. Create different learning centers related to "Things at Home." See page 5 for learning center ideas.

5. Lead students in a discussion regarding their favorite rooms at home. Ask them what it is in that room that makes it their favorite. Have students draw detailed pictures of their favorite rooms. Explain that the edges of the paper are the edges of the rooms they choose. Have a prepared example displayed on the bulletin board entitled "I'm Home!" See page 76 for more information on bulletin board construction.

6. Lead students in a discussion of things that do not belong in a house (a truck, a whale, etc.) Ask students why these things do not belong.

In a People House *(cont.)*

Suggested Activities *(cont.)*

Setting the Stage *(cont.)*

7. Have fun with your students in this Concentration-style game. Students should be seated in a circle. One student begins the game by completing the sentence "Our home has a _____ in it." The next student states the previously mentioned item and a different item. For example, "Our home has a _____ and a _____ in it." The objective of the game is to increase memory skills of students through the identification of household items. (If this is too difficult for your students, have them draw pictures of their item to hold up in front of them.) Eventually a long list of items will be formed, with each student adding to the list as the game goes on.

8. Have students bring something to school from their bedrooms at home to share with the class. (See the permission letter on page 67.)

9. Ask students to complete this statement: "If I were a (type of animal), my home would look like. . ." Change animals for different students.

10. Have students build their own homes out of tangrams or other classroom items, first individually and then in groups.

Enjoying the Book

1. As you read the book, have the students note words that sound the same. Identify these as rhyming words. Write three sets of rhyming words on sentence strips. Have students place rhyming words together on the chalk ledge or pocket chart. Open up discussion for other sets of rhyming words.

2. Count sets of rhyming words in the book. Explain to students that there are many more things in our homes besides what was mentioned by Mr. Bird and Mr. Mouse in the story. Have students each draw a picture of something inside their homes. Take dictation of what the students say is in their houses.

3. Have students look at certain pages where alliteration is used, such as "banana, bathtub, bottles, brooms." Ask students what they notice about those four words. Lead students to realize that each word begins with the letter "b." Continue with other pages.

Extending the Book

1. Cut pictures from magazines that show different items we have at home. Students can classify these pictures in one of two ways. Option 1: Use two shoeboxes, one in which to place items that belong at home, and the other for those that do not. Option 2: Use several boxes, each representing a room in a house. Place bathroom pictures in the bathroom box, kitchen pictures in the kitchen box, etc.

In a People House *(cont.)*

Suggested Activities *(cont.)*

Extending the Book *(cont.)*

2. Home Graph: Ask students to think about how their homes look on the outside. Place pictures of one-story and two-story homes, a condo/apartment, a mobile home, and an "other" category in columns on the chalkboard. For pictures, see Flannel Pieces on page 20. Students should be given a smaller version of each picture. Direct students to color and cut out the one that looks the most like their home. Graph these results on the board by taping each student's home in the correct column. Lead the class towards drawing conclusions regarding the graph. (What kind of home do most students live in? How do you know?)

3. Discuss the home as a place where families live. Note with students how not all families look the same. Discuss different people who are all part of the same family, such as stepparents, grandparents, sisters, uncles, etc.

4. Allow students to share with each other all the people who live in their home by taking the time to draw them. The Family Portrait activity on page 9 allows students to express a part of themselves they can be proud of—their families. Set aside time to let each student share his or her family portrait.

5. After completing this activity, have students punch two holes in the circles at the top of the page. Thread a string through the holes and hang pictures on the wall or make a bulletin board entitled "In a People House" (page 75).

6. Discuss with students what they think their houses might look like without electricity. Guide students to realize that there would be no lamps, microwaves, TVs, refrigerators, etc.

7. Provide students with visual aids, through Flannel Pieces on page 12 and 13, of homes from the early 1900s to show how people used to live with iceboxes, fireplaces for cooking, and candles for light. Discuss how these items have been replaced by the electric items of today, and explain how these "new" machines make things easier for people.

8. Ask students to draw what their homes would look like if there were no electricity. Use "Yesterday and Today" homes on page 14.

9. Make a "Yesterday and Today" bulletin board where items of today, such as a car or microwave oven, are placed on the today side. Likewise, a carriage or stove should be placed on yesterday's side. See the Unit Management section on page 74 for bulletin board construction.

10. This activity will provide students with practice in identifying beginning phonetic sounds of objects around the house. Have students think of something in a certain room of the house, for example, the kitchen. One student might volunteer "sink." Ask students which letter is at the beginning of that word. Write the word on the board. Continue in the same manner with a few more examples.

11. Have students classify the household objects on page 10.

Family Portrait

Directions: Draw a picture inside the frame of all the people who live in your house.

Organize It!

Directions: Reproduce this page and page 11. Cut up the cards. Have students place the cards into the rooms they believe the objects on the cards belong in.

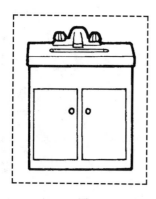

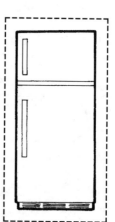

Organize It! *(cont.)*

Flannel Pieces

Yesterday and Today

Directions: Construct flannel pieces for visual aids. (You may wish to enlarge the objects below before doing so.) For directions on how to construct flannel pieces, see the Unit Management section on page 72. For use with the bulletin board, see page 74.

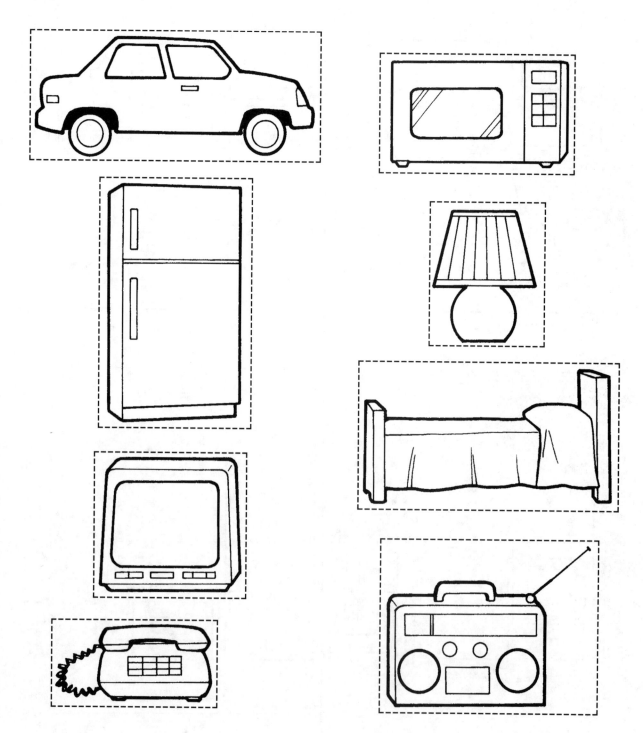

Flannel Pieces *(cont.)*

Yesterday and Today

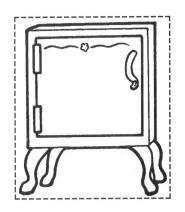

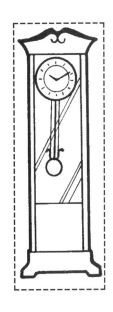

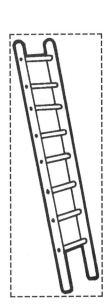

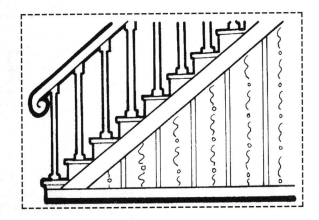

Yesterday and Today

Homes

Directions: Draw a picture of the inside of your home as it is today.

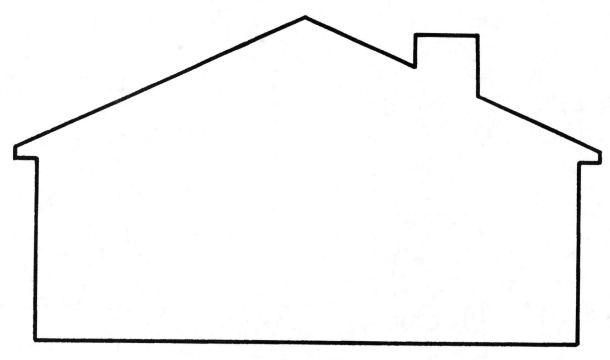

Next, pretend there is no electricity, and draw what the inside of your home would look like.

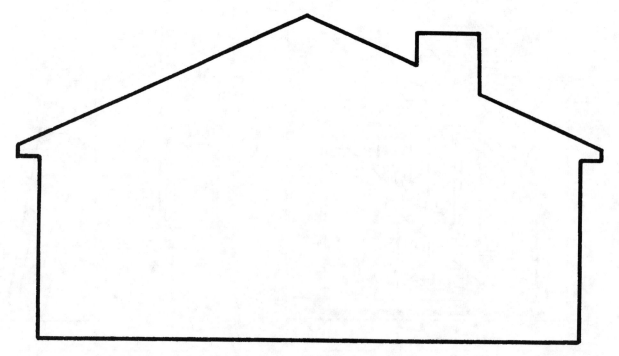

Match-Up

Directions: Match and then draw a circle around the groups that have the same number of things found in a people house.

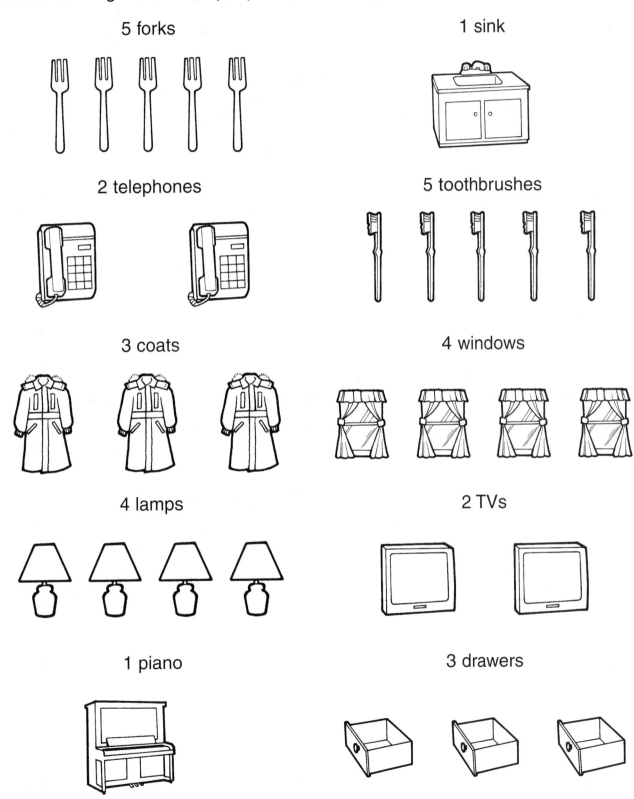

5 forks

1 sink

2 telephones

5 toothbrushes

3 coats

4 windows

4 lamps

2 TVs

1 piano

3 drawers

Letter Hunt!

Directions: Look for objects at home that begin with one of the letters in the magnifying glass. What did you find? On this page draw what you found in the magnifying glass.

Something's Fishy

Directions: Circle the things that do not belong in this people house. How many did you find? Write the number in the box at the bottom of the page.

How many did you find?

Let's Make Big Books

Finish *In a People House* by having students make a class Big Book entitled "In a(n) [preschool's name] House."

Students will create the class big book, using pattern on page 19. Enlarge the patterns. Pass out the enlarged house pattern, instructing students to use crayons and markers to color their own homes. Explain that the edges of the paper are the edges of the homes. It is helpful to hand these pages out after they have already been cut so that the students can better visualize and illustrate their homes. Some students will draw the outside, some the inside. Allow for variation. (Practice pages may be helpful, depending on the students.) Ask students to describe to you what is happening in their pictures. Take dictations of their stories. It may be helpful to have another person available to take notes, or this part of the project could be done in learning centers.

Bind pages together, placing the dictation on the back of the preceeding page, so that students' stories face their pictures. For ideas on how to bind the big book, see the Unit Management section, page 73. Place a cover on the front and a short author's page in the back. For the author's page, use another enlarged home pattern page and place students' pictures on it with a description of the class, such as the following:

This book was put together by [teacher's name]'s class of hardworking [grade level]. They enjoy [playing outside, eating pizza, Nintendo, etc.].
When they grow up, they would like to be [teachers, doctors, bus drivers, nurses, etc.].

This book was put together by Ms. Levin's first grade class.

House Big Book Pattern

Directions: Enlarge the house pattern for each student in class. Color the cover page only. For construction of a big book, see the Unit Management section, page 73.

cover page pattern

student page pattern

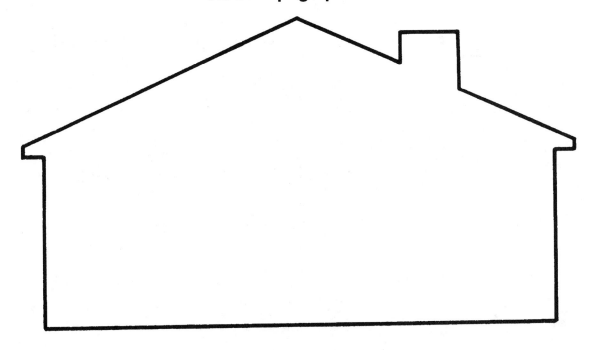

Flannel Pieces

Different Kinds of Homes

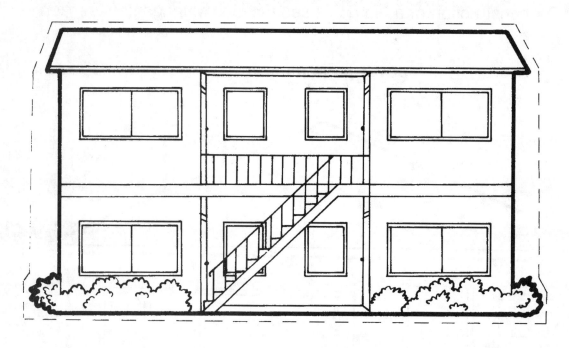

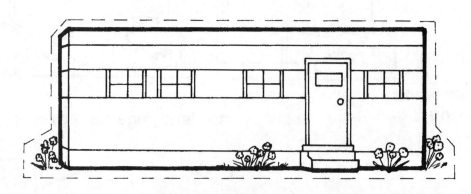

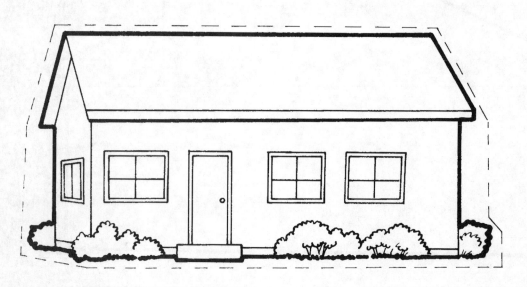

Flannel Pieces *(cont.)*

Different Kinds of Homes *(cont.)*

A House for Hermit Crab
by Eric Carle
Summary

In this book Eric Carle paints a picture of a busy little hermit crab who works all year long decorating and gathering treasures for his shell. Come December, Hermit realizes that he has grown and it is time to move to another shell. Hermit is overjoyed when he realizes he has the chance to decorate all over again. This book encourages children to see that change brings exciting possibilities.

Suggested Activities

Setting the Stage

1. Explain to students that they will continue to learn about all different kinds of homes. Ask students to tell you what other kinds of homes there are. Accept and list all different kinds of responses.

2. Allow students to preview the book by first reading aloud the title and predicting what will happen based on picture clues.

3. Create different learning centers. See Learning Centers on page 5 for ideas.

4. Display the classroom bulletin board "Our Treasures from Home," to be completed with student work later. See the Unit Management section on page 77 for construction ideas.

5. Briefly discuss the information regarding sea life found on the front and back pages of *A House for Hermit Crab*. Provide visual aids for the students, magazine pictures and/or illustrations included in the book.

6. Ask students if they have ever had to move to a new house before. Allow them to share what that experience felt like.

Enjoying the Book

1. As you read the book, have students carefully watch the size of Hermit and note what is happening to him. If appropriate, start a class growth chart showing how tall the students have grown throughout the year. This can be done by designating an area with a sheet of butcher paper hung lengthwise. Write "On the Grow" at the top and simply mark and date the height of each student once a month.

2. While reading the book, ask students to think of what time of year it is for Hermit. List the months of the year with a distinguishing picture nearby, and refer to the chart briefly while reading to help teach the order of the months.

3. While reading the story, add to a board flannel pieces to be counted at the end of the story. See Flannel Pieces on pages 26 and 27. For construction of flannel pieces, check the Unit Management section on page 72.

A House for Hermit Crab (cont.)

Suggested Activities (cont.)

Enjoying the Book (cont.)

Ask students how Hermit felt when he had to leave his home. Discuss how he felt when he found a new home. Encourage students to notice that Hermit liked the change.

This is a story your class will want to reread, so feel free to do so!

Extending the Book

1. Discuss with students that not all homes look the same. Have students complete Let's Go Home! on page 29 by placing the animals in their correct homes.

2. Enlarge the chart and complete the Year at a Glance class activity on page 32. As you reread the story, attach a picture from page 26 of the sea life Hermit encountered that month. Next to the name of the month, add a brief sentence telling what Hermit collected for his home. Although students may be at a pre-reading level, it is important for writing to be modeled for them as a key skill. The added pictures help in determining meaning. As a variation, give students the chance to write their own charts. Before enlarging the chart on page 32, make enough copies for the entire class. In learning centers, have students sketch their own pictures of what Hermit collected that month and write in either the name of the sea life or their own sentences.

3. Have students decorate their own hermit homes on page 33, using classroom extras such as buttons, yarn, fabric pieces, sand, etc. Hermit was proud of how his home looked, so your students will be, too!

4. Use the flannel pieces on page 26 to re-enact the story. This is a good activity to develop sequencing skills in your students.

5. Have students draw a picture of something at home that is important to them. Students should dictate a sentence about why that object is important to them. Have students draw their items in the treasure chest on page 34.

6. Display the picture on Our Treasures From Home! board. See the Unit Management section on page 77 for bulletin board construction.

7. Reread the part of the story where Hermit meets the snails (in June). Explain that the snails were going to help keep Hermit's house clean. Ask students what kind of jobs they do to keep their homes clean. When you work, do you do your best? Do you use kind words?

8. Set up nine special learning centers for housework experiences. Students should be given the opportunity to gain a sense of independence and autonomy by performing various jobs commonly done at home.

   Suggested Activities: wash play dishes or paintbrushes, pick up trash, clean desks, sweep floor, scrub sink, sharpen pencils, straighten books, clean erasers, straighten desks and chairs, etc.

   Discuss how it felt to work together as a team to help clean up "our house."

A House for Hermit Crab (cont.)

Suggested Activities (cont.)

Extending the Book (cont.)

9. Have students draw a picture of one job they do to help at home like the snails at Hermit's home. Enlarge and use the snail-shaped pattern on page 33. Bind the pages together in a class book entitled "At Home I . . ." For ideas on how to bind class books, see page 73.

10. Discuss with students that our home is a place of shelter from the weather. Ask: What does the outside of your home look like? Use Flannel Pieces on page 28 for students' answers. Have students tell you what part of the house protects them from rain (roof), wind (walls), dirt and germs (floor). What part of your house lets you go in and out (door)? lets light in (windows)? lets smoke from the fireplace out (chimney)?

11. Copy Flannel Pieces on page 28. Pass out a part to each student. Have students work in pairs or in larger groups, depending on students' ages, to build their own homes.

12. Have students make their classroom into a home for another little creature. See Worm Wiggle Home on page 25.

13. Introduce students to this song sung to the tune of "BINGO." Students love the chance to sing in class!

1 There is a place where I can go,
   (*Students should use hand gestures throughout the song.*)

2 and yes I love it so-o!
   (*Place hand over eyes as if searching for line 1.*)

3 (My) H-O-U-S-E
   (*Place hands crossed over chest for line 2.*)

4 H-O-U-S-E

5 H-O-U-S-E
   (*Place fingertips together to form a roof for lines 3–6.*)

6 (My) House is its name-o!

As a variation of the song, use students' names.

> There is a place where we can go,
> and yes we love it so-o!
> (Jenna's) H-O-U-S-E
> H-O-U-S-E
> (Jenna's) H-O-U-S-E
> (Jenna's) House is its name-o!

Worm Wiggle Home

Below are the directions for turning two plastic two-liter bottles, newspapers, potting soil, and crackers into a worm home.

Materials:

- two plastic two-liter bottles
- shredded newspaper
- potting soil
- soda crackers, carrot or apple skins, etc. (See Directions, #6)
- common earthworms
- water

Directions:

1. Cut the tops off both two-liter bottles right above where the label would begin.
2. Place one bottle aside.
3. Shred newspaper into one-inch (2.54 cm) strips. Place in water until soaked. Wring out slightly.
4. Put handful of potting soil on top of shredded newspapers.
5. Add earthworms.
6. Feed with soda crackers, carrot skins, apple skins, or anything that won't rot too quickly.
7. Poke holes in the bottom of the other bottle for air.
8. Finally, place other bottle upside-down over the top of the worm home. Air holes should be on top.

Flannel Pieces

A House for Hermit Crab

Flannel Pieces *(cont.)*

A House for Hermit Crab (cont.)

Flannel Pieces *(cont.)*

Home Parts

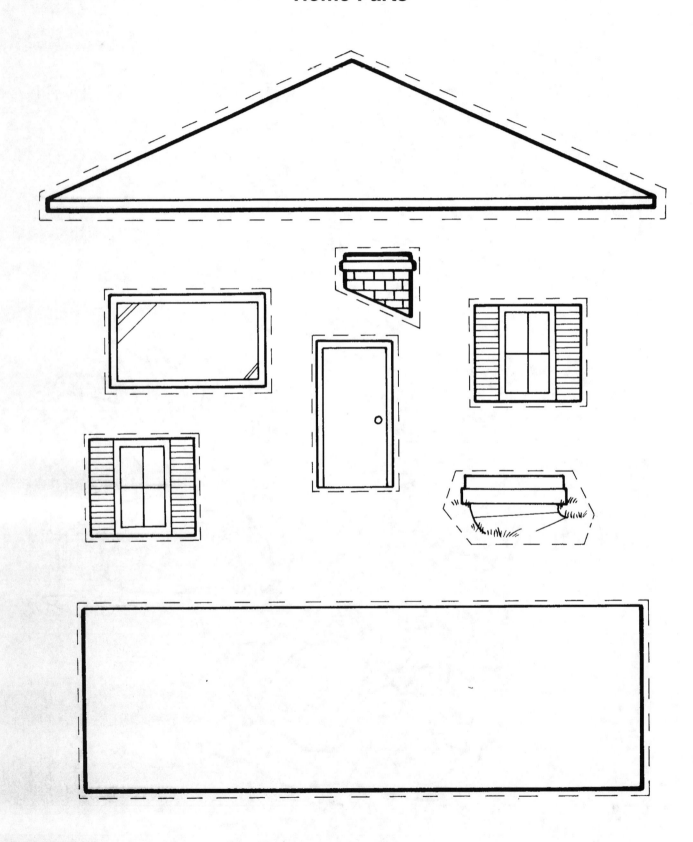

Let's Go Home!

Directions: Put the animals on this page into their homes on page 30. First color, then cut and paste.

Let's Go Home! *(cont.)*

Home Collections

Directions: Draw a picture of the things in your house that are wider than you, thinner than you, taller than you, and shorter than you in each box. Write the name of what you drew on the line at the bottom of the box.

wider than me	thinner than me
_____	
taller than me	
	_____
	shorter than me
_____	_____

Year at a Glance

Directions: Make enough copies for each student, and then enlarge the following chart. With a pen, draw a picture and/or write a sentence of what Hermit saw each month. Model the importance of writing for your students, and if necessary add a simple sketch for meaning.

January: Hermit saw a_____.
February:
March:
April:
May:
June:
July:
August:
September:
October:
November:
December:

Home Decorator

Directions: Decorate Hermit's home below with color, yarn, sand, buttons, etc. Be creative! Or, enlarge this pattern for a class big book called "At Home I . . ." to show the kinds of jobs students do at home. (See Extending the Book # 9, page 24.)

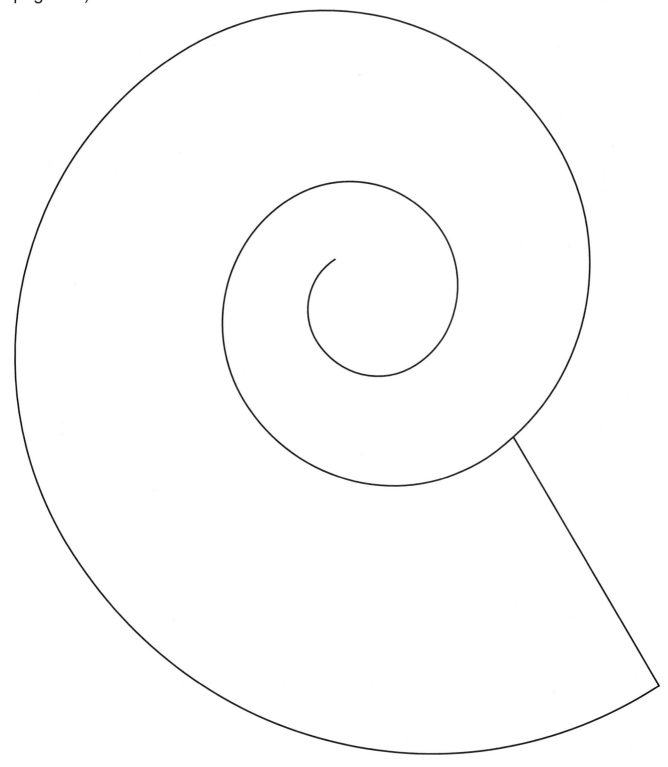

Our Treasures from Home!

Directions: Inside the treasure chest, draw something that you treasure at home. Finish the sentence at the bottom of the page.

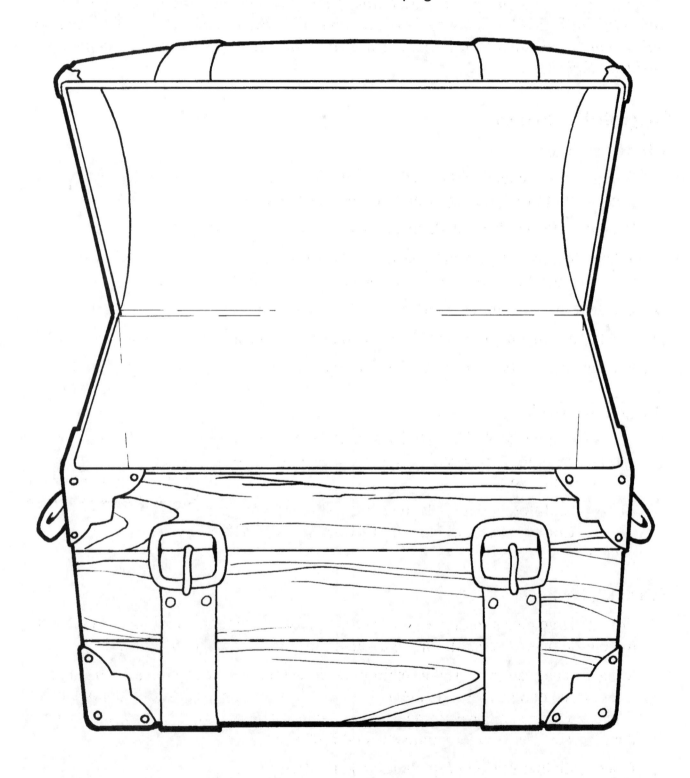

I treasure my_____.

The Fourth Little Pig

by Teresa Celsi

(This section of the unit can be used with other versions of The Three Little Pigs.)

Summary

This story is a cute spin-off of the traditional tale of The Three Little Pigs. *In this colorfully illustrated book, the sister of the three little pigs comes along to help the pigs realize that even though their house is strong and safe, there is so much to see and do outside of their home.*

Suggested Activities

Setting the Stage

1. Explain to students that they will continue to learn about homes; this time they will learn about three little pigs who built their own homes.

2. Read the title and have students predict who the fourth little pig might be.

3. Take a picture-walk through the story. Allow students to predict what they think might happen based on what is happening in the pictures.

4. Create different learning centers. See Learning Centers on page 5.

5. Lead a discussion on the kinds of materials from which homes are built.

6. For fun and artistic expression, have students draw a house using only curvy lines.

Enjoying the Book

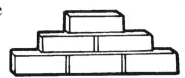

1. As you read the book, have students think quietly about the parts of the story they were not able to predict. Discuss at the end of the story.

2. List all the different materials the pigs used to build their homes. Complete with Extending the Book Activity #10, page 36.

Extending the Book

1. Provide large boxes for students to use while role-playing the traditional story of the three little pigs. (Popcorn for the audience makes this activity delightful!)

2. Students can read their way to building their own homes. Use pieces from Build Your Home on page 46. This is perfect for a learning center or file-folder game. When students can correctly read a word, letter, or math fact, they earn a piece of their house. The reading continues until each student's house is built.

3. Practice dialing 911 on prop phones and on page 38.

The Fourth Little Pig *(cont.)*

Suggested Activities *(cont.)*

Enjoying the Book *(cont.)*

Topics:

4. Discuss how our homes are places where we need to feel safe.

   Use some of the topics listed.

   - **Fire safety:** stop, drop, and roll
   - **911:** emergency phone number
   - **Power Loss:** When all lights go out, stop, rest, and wait for an adult with a flashlight.
   - **Earthquake:** Hide under a strong table holding one table leg and the other hand on back of neck.

   - **Matches:** Never touch them. Get an adult to pick them up.
   - **Stranger at your door:** Never open the door. An adult can open the door for you.
   - **Call your local fire and police department for more details on staying safe at home.**

5. Send a letter home regarding student's study of safety at home to continue with the practicing of their phone numbers. See Letters Home starting on page 66. Give treats to those who can repeat their phone number to you. Encourage students to give phone numbers only to a safe adult like a teacher or police officer for help.

6. Discuss with students whom they might invite to their homes and why. Explain the vocabulary words "invite" and "invitation." Ask students what they might talk about with that person.

7. Have students design their own signs welcoming families to come and visit them. Complete by punching holes in the signs to hang them at home with parents' help. See Welcome Home on page 39.

8. Encourage students to recognize patterns of colors and shapes on a colored and enlarged Home Pattern on page 40. They should see patterns in the colors of homes, sizes of homes, windows, people on the sidewalk, cars on the streets, trees out front, etc.

9. Copy and pass out the Home Pattern on page 41. Have students make their own patterns on the homes and sidewalk. Make sure your visual is placed where students can observe it. Monitor students by asking them where they are making patterns. Suggest more complicated patterns when appropriate.

10. Discuss how different people use different things to build their homes out of. Show pictures of homes from around the world made from brick, wood, stone, dirt, grass, ice, straw, banana leaves, etc. See the flannel pieces on page 50.

The Fourth Little Pig (cont.)

Suggested Activities (cont.)

Extending the Book (cont.)

11. Have students pretend they could build a house from anything: pillows, pizza, chocolate chips, toys, etc. You may want to suggest a few options, then graph the results for the class.

12. Make homes from magazine pictures of food, furniture, etc. Pass out old magazines for students to cut out pictures. Have students use these pictures to make their own unique homes by pasting them onto white paper. If desired, arrange these homes on butcher paper to hang on the wall. Now your students have their own unique neighborhood.

13. Divide the class into "construction crews." Each student should have a colored name tag (page 49) to identify their crew. The crews should work cooperatively to build a house from blocks. (Shoeboxes or math-manipulative cubes can be a good alternative.) Next, have the groups make houses from pliable straws and tape. Since this is a challenging but fun activity, have awards, (page 49) for each construction crew's house, such as tallest house, smallest house, most wobbly home, etc. Accept student ideas for award topics.

14. Use game cards from page 42 and 43 to play Match-Up. Turn over colored and laminated cards and take turns trying to find a pair.

brick home

home on stilts

15. Use the game cards to play "Go Home," a game in the style of "Go Fish." Two students may ask each other for a match, and if no match is found, the student draws from the deck.

911

Directions: Color the phone and practice dialing 911 for emergency. Trace the emergency numbers on the bottom of the page.

Welcome Home

Directions: Decorate your welcome sign. Trace the word "Welcome" onto it to invite family and friends over to visit.

Home Pattern: Teacher Edition

Directions: Color and enlarge to make a visual aid for students. Use as many patterns as possible in your coloring and decorating.

Home Pattern: Student Edition

Directions: Color the homes of the three little pigs to make your own pattern.
Add more patterns by completing the street scene.

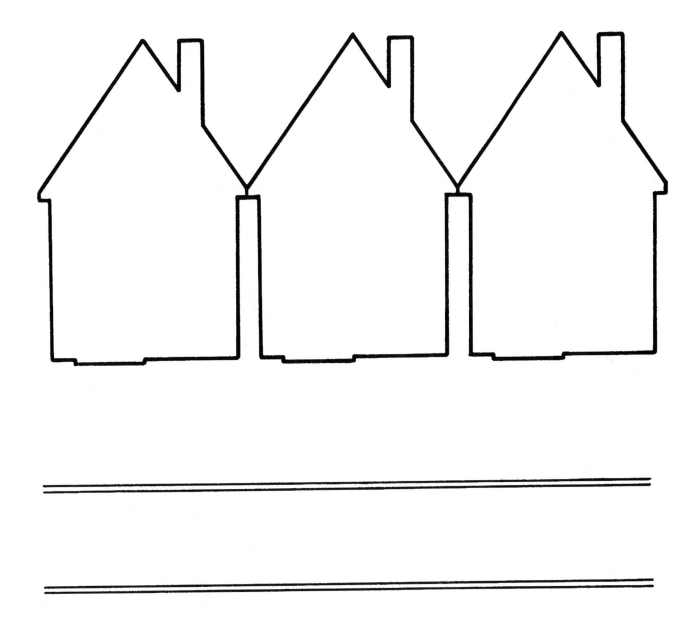

Game Cards

Make two or four copies of the game cards pattern. Color, cut, and laminate to play different games. See Extending the Book on page 37 for ideas.

grass home

apartment home

mud home

home on stilts

Game Cards *(cont.)*

brick home

stone home

wood home

ice home

Homes on a Street

Directions: Count the homes on each street. Write the number in the box. Cut the strips out and paste them, on a separate piece of paper, in order from the least number of homes to the most.

Made From . . .

Directions: Draw a line to match the home to what it was made from. Color.

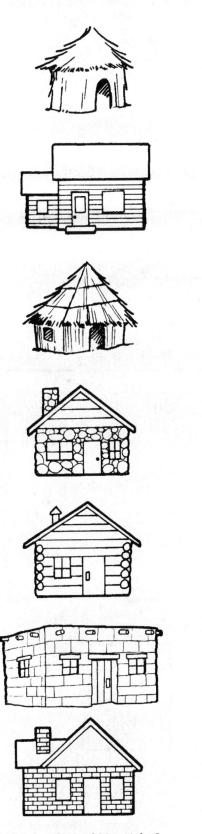

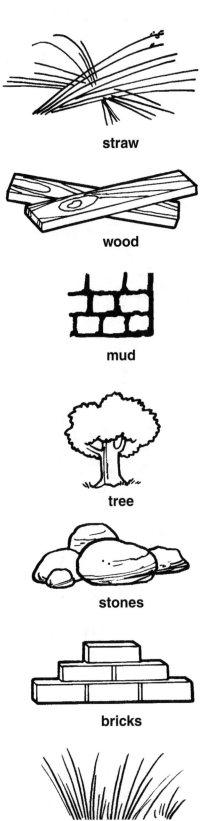

Build Your Home

Directions: Students should identify words on flash cards. Some flash cards have been provided on pages 47 and 48. (If desired, use your own flash cards of letters, shapes, colors, numbers, etc.) With each correct identification the student earns a part of the home. These can be glued to another sheet of construction paper, or just placed on the students' desks. Continue until the home is built.

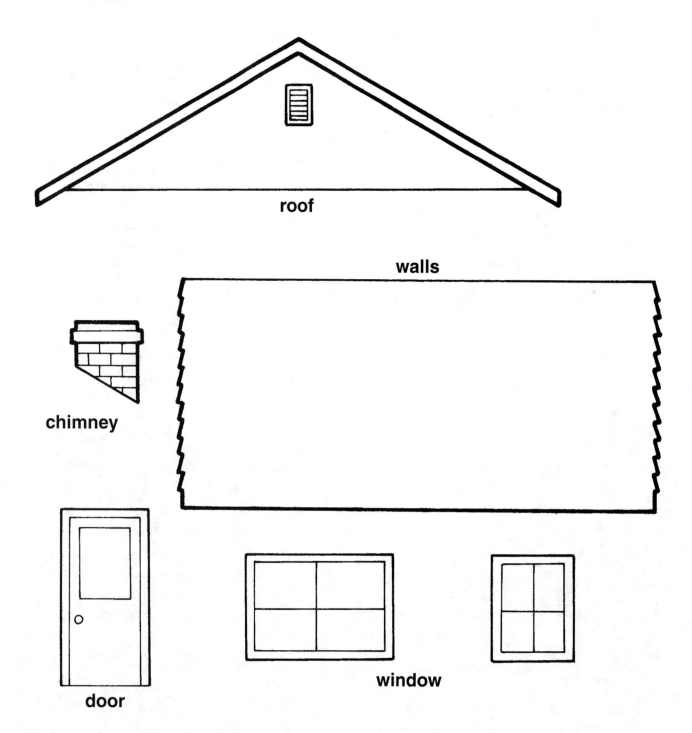

roof

walls

chimney

door

window

Building Your Home Flash Cards

house	**bath**
roof	**tub**
door	**sink**

Building Your Home Flash Cards *(cont.)*

window	**wall**
floor	**home**
yard	**room**

Construction Crew Name Tags

Copy the hard-hat pattern below onto different-colored construction paper for different class groups. Pin them to students.

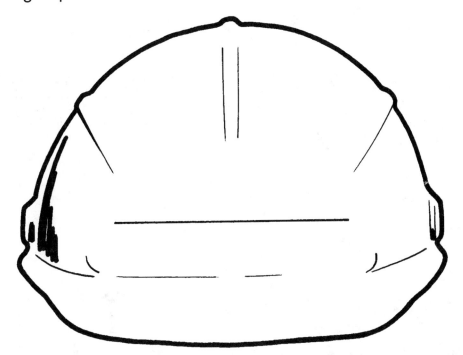

Construction Crew Awards

Give one to each group when its home is built. Copy these onto the same color groups used for name tags.

Built from Flannel Pieces

Use the following flannel pieces to illustrate different building materials used around the world. For ideas on how to construct flannel pieces, see the Unit Management section, page 72.

Where Do I Belong?

Directions: Cut out the pieces at the bottom of the page. Match the large door, tree, and person to the large house. Match the others to the smaller-sized homes in which they belong. Color.

Unlock It

Directions: Unlock the door with the right key. To find the right key, match the capital letter on the door to the lowercase letter on the key. Draw a line to match them together.

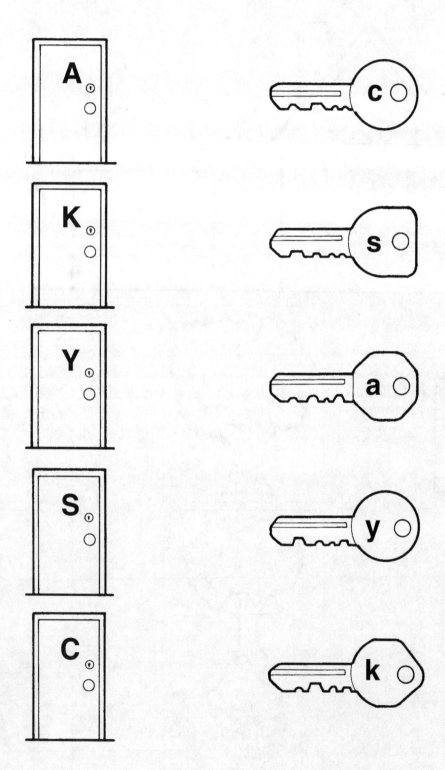

Home Sweet Home

Use classroom discussion and the following hands-on activity to help students review the major concepts they have learned throughout this unit. (**Note:** This is a great activity to invite parents to participate in.

Classroom Discussion Ideas: Discuss the parts of the house: walls, roof, windows, chimneys, etc. Allow students to suggest materials that would be used to make a wall, such as brick, wood, grass, etc. Take time to review with students what they have learned about homes thus far.

Hands-On Activity: Now the fun begins! This activity can get messy, so cover tables with butcher paper. Ingredients should be divided into table-groups or other appropriate groups. You should make enough frosting for the class, and divide the frosting among the groups. Furnish paper plates with each student's name written on his or her plate and hand them out accordingly. Each table should have different plates or bowls with assorted goodies in them, as well as a supply of frosting per every two students. The plastic knives can be used to spread the frosting onto the carton and graham crackers. Begin to construct homes by first placing frosting on the bottom of the milk carton and then generously covering all sides of the carton. Place graham crackers on first. Allow time for students to decorate with candy goodies, using the frosting as glue. You'll be surprised at the creativity and knowledge they will demonstrate.

Ingredients (serves approximatly 20 students)

- small milk carton (one per student)
- two packages red hots
- two packages gumdrops
- five packages Life Savers
- colored candy sprinkles
- red string licorice
- pretzel sticks
- large package M&M's
- two boxes powdered sugar
- one 8–10 ounce milk carton per student

- mixer for frosting*
- measuring spoons
- miniature Tootsie Rolls
- colored mini marshmallows
- 25 plastic knives (one per student)
- 25 large paper plates (one per student)
- two boxes graham crackers
- mini candy canes
- Necco wafers
- two cans meringue powder
- four to five bowls (one per table)

Homemade frosting is easier to spread and hardens more like cement to hold goodies in place, but other frosting can be used.

Frosting for Graham-Cracker Houses

- one 16-ounce package powdered sugar
- three tablespoons meringue powder
- $\frac{1}{3}$ cup warm water

In bowl, with mixer at low speed, beat powdered sugar, meringue powder, and $\frac{1}{3}$ cup warm water about seven minutes, until mixture is stiff and knife drawn through it leaves a clean-cut path. Makes about three cups.

Me on the Map
by Joan Sweeney

Summary

Written in the first person, this colorfully illustrated book provides a frame of reference for students in understanding where their homes are in relation to their neighborhood, state, and even country. In the book, an adorable young girl discovers that she herself has a place on the map, showing that each person, has special place in the world. This is a great introduction to helping young students begin to think of things in a more global sense.

Suggested Activities

Setting the Stage

1. Allow students to preview the book by first reading the title aloud and showing them the pictures. Discuss with students what they think the story will be about.

2. Create different learning centers related to the theme. See Learning Centers on page 5.

3. Display the bulletin board for This Is Our Neighborhood (page 78). See Unit Management on page 78 for bulletin board construction.

4. Discuss with students the meaning of the word "neighborhood." Lead students to an understanding that their neighborhood is made up of many different houses and places where people live and work.

5. Encourage students to discuss what their neighborhood looks like. Are there many trees? Are there buses that drive around? Are there any parks? What kinds of restaurants or stores do you see in your neighborhood? Are there apartments? Are there churches?

6. Discuss with students what a map is. Bring in a map, preferably one large enough for all the students to see, and show students where they are on the map. (The social studies teacher may have a map available to use if you do not.)

Enjoying the Book

1. List with students all the different types of maps that were made in the story (room, house, street, town, state, country, and world).

2. Have students look carefully at the illustrations. Ask them to find the young girl's house on her street, her street on the map of her town, and her town on the map of her state.

3. Discuss with students the kinds of things that are in the girl's town according to the illustration. Have students tell whether or not the same kinds of things are in their town (for example, cows, factories, a river, etc.).

Me on the Map *(cont.)*

Suggested Activities *(cont.)*

Extending the Book

1. If possible, take a walk around the neighborhood, discussing what you see. For example, if you see a bank, discuss the purpose of the bank. You may want to take a camera with you to take pictures of all the things you see. If this is not possible, bring paper and pencil to make a list of the community buildings you find. Arrangements must be made within your school district's guidelines for completing this activity. (Permission slips and chaperons may be required.)

2. When you have completed walking around the neighborhood, display pictures, photographs or drawings so students can view their neighborhood. Place above the pictures the title "This is our neighborhood."

3. Discuss with students the necessity of keeping their neighborhood free of litter and trash. Ask them to think about what their neighborhood would look like if everyone threw down a piece of trash. Discuss the importance of recycling our trash so that we have less of it to fill up our garbage dumps.

4. Show students the illustration of the young girl's map of the room. Encourage beginning mapping skills by guiding your students to make maps of their own rooms at home. Explain to students that a map is made as if you were looking down at what you were drawing, like a bug on the ceiling. Help students think of things that are in their rooms at home. Tell them they first need to make a box and leave a space where the door would go. (Demonstrate on chalk/white board for students to see.) Next, ask if there are any windows in their rooms. Color a blue rectangle to show a window. Next, have students draw where their beds are, and continue with other objects that might be in their rooms. Encourage students to try to put all their items in the right place, but allow for questions due to the fact that this may be the student's first experience with making a simple map. It should include no more than three to four items for preschool-age students. Older students can have more detail if you feel it is appropriate. Finally, make sure that students draw themselves in their rooms.

5. Have students color in maps of their rooms and frame them on colored construction paper. Display these pieces of art in the classroom under the title "Me in My Room" or "My First Map." Parents will be impressed with the students' hard work.

6. Bring in a map of your neighborhood. If possible, pin or staple the map to the wall. Place pins with tags on them, page 58, to show where each of the community buildings is. It is possible to do this activity using only the street names of each student's neighborhood. Use the Neighborhood Map letter on page 69 for parents' permission; however, if all parents do not agree to allow that kind of information, then this activity can be done using only community buildings.

Me on the Map (cont.)

Extending the Book (cont.)

7. Discuss with students the kinds of jobs people do to keep their neighborhood running. (See the bibiography on page 79 for books to read about community workers.) Use "People at Work" on page 59.

8. Ask students to draw a picture of the kind of work they would like to do when they are old enough. Use "I Want To Be . . ." on page 60.

9. Encourage beginning writing skills by using "Hello from _____!" on page 61. Students should make postcards from their own neighborhood. Have them write, or copy from the board, a brief message saying hello to a friend or family member. (If your class has pen-pal connections to a different school, this is the perfect way to write to them. If you have not connected to another school through pen pals, now is the perfect time to start!) Have students turn over their postcards and draw a picture of something that is representative of their city (e.g., a monument, a local crop, etc.). Make sure they leave space in the corner for a stamp. Finally, if students are able to address a postcard, help them do that—otherwise, leave the address blank so that a parent can help them send it from home.

> Hello!
>
> from,
> Sharon!
>
> | Chis Mac
> | 833 Alex Rd.
> | Short Beach, NY
> | 12345
>
> Place Stamp Here!

10. See Home Connections on page 71 for further ideas.

11. Culminating Activity: Our School

Discuss with students the importance of their school in their neighborhood. Explain to them that it is the place where people can learn to be anything they would like to be. Have students continue their learning of mapping skills by mapping one of the most important places in their neighborhood—their school.

Set aside enough time for your class to go on a walk around your school. Make sure that you see all the important places such as the playground, cafeteria, principal's office, music room, computer room, and library.

Enlarge the Our School Patterns on page 62 and 63 in order to put together your own map of the school on a large sheet of butcher paper. Once the patterns have been enlarged and cut out, and butcher paper is temporarily posted, have the students sit around your map and place each of patterns where they go in relation to your classroom. Your classroom should be glued down first in order to give your students a frame of reference. Use a black marker to make pathways/hallways showing where the students walked. After all the patterns are in place, allow students to decorate your map by coloring the buildings, adding children to the yard, and placing trees around the edges of the school. This map should be posted on the classroom wall and titled "Our School."

Neighborhood 3-2-1 Hike!

Directions: Walk around your neighborhood with a safe adult, such as a family member or friend, and write down the names and numbers of all the different things you see! In the last space, draw something that you saw, and write the name and number of times you saw it.

Our Neighborhood

Copy and cut out the arrow tags below to use on your community map. Color in the pictures for added effect.

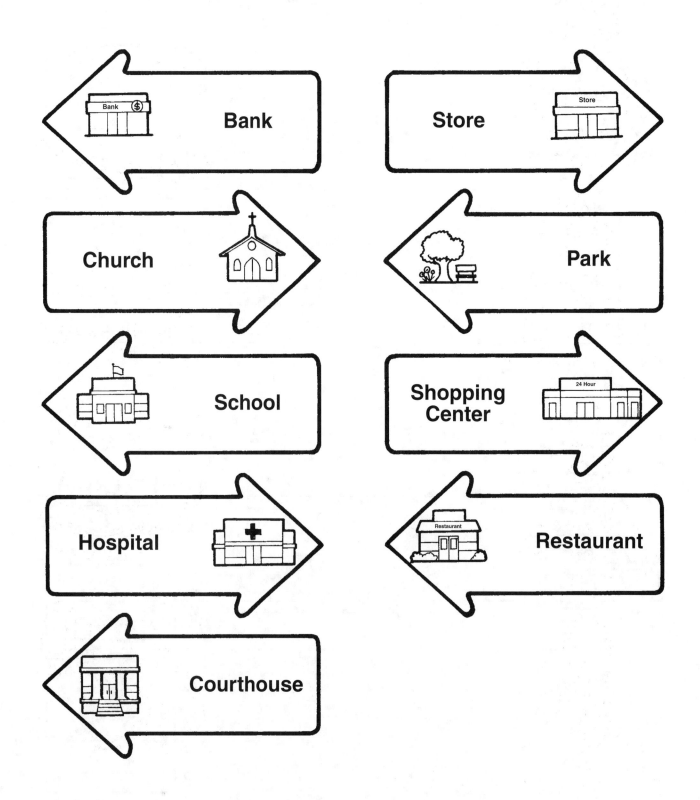

People at Work

Directions: Match community workers to the tools they need to get their jobs done. Trace the name of the worker under each picture. Color.

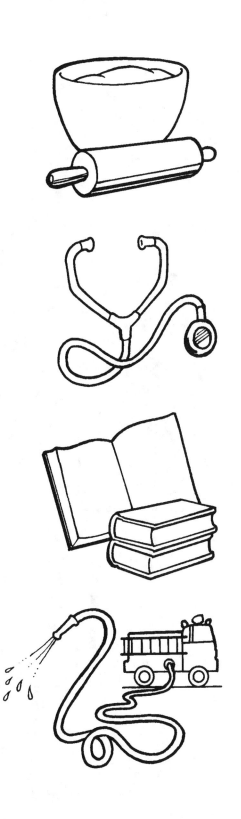

I Want To Be . . .

Directions: Draw a picture of the job you would like to do when you get older. Make sure that you draw all the tools you will need to get that job done. Color it in. Write the name of what you would like to be at the bottom of the page.

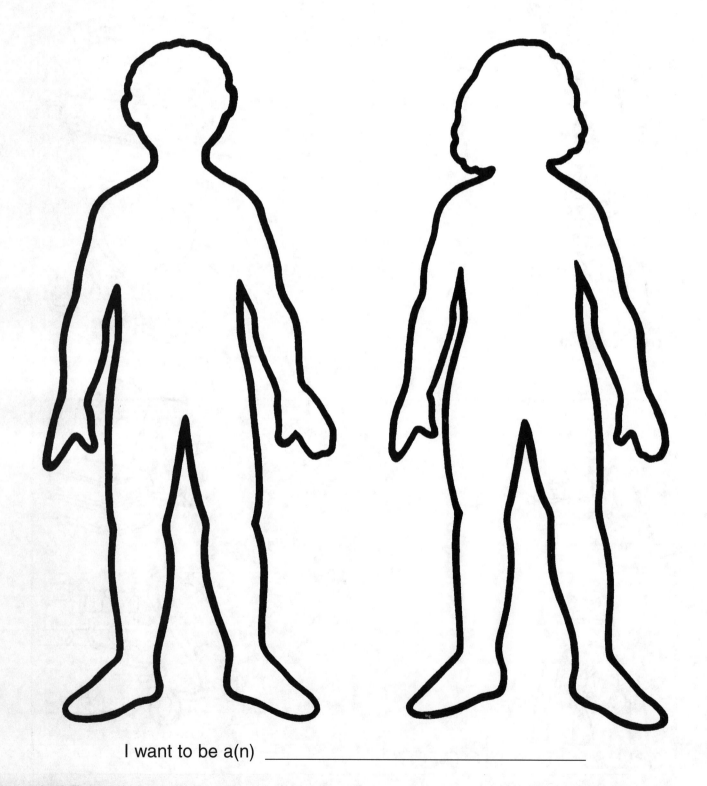

I want to be a(n) _____

Hello from_____!

Directions: Cut out the front and back of the postcard below. On the front, draw a picture of something in your neighborhood. On the back, write a message to someone special. Next, place the postcard on a piece of cardboard and trace around it in pencil; then cut it out. Attach the front and back to either side of the postcard.

Front

Back

Dear _____,

From,

_____

Our School Patterns

Enlarge and cut out the patterns below for use with Our School on page 56. Once the patterns are glued down on butcher paper for the school map, have students help color in the buildings.

Our School Patterns *(cont.)*

Flannel Pieces/Bulletin Board

Community Buildings

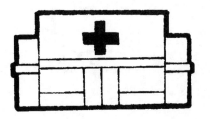

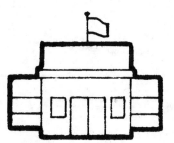

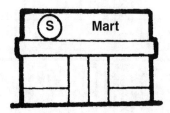

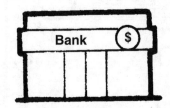

Flannel Pieces/Bulletin Board *(cont.)*

Community Buildings *(cont.)*

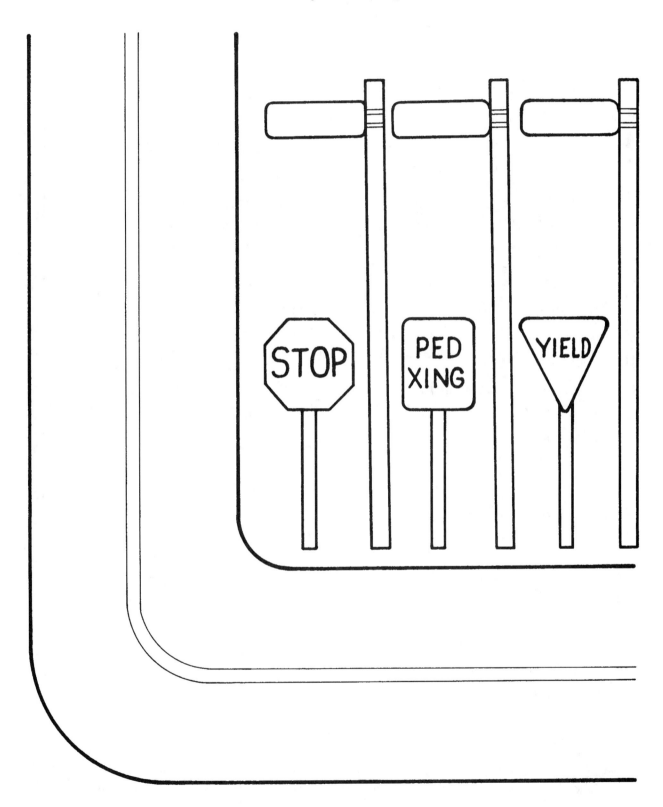

Unit Introduction Letter

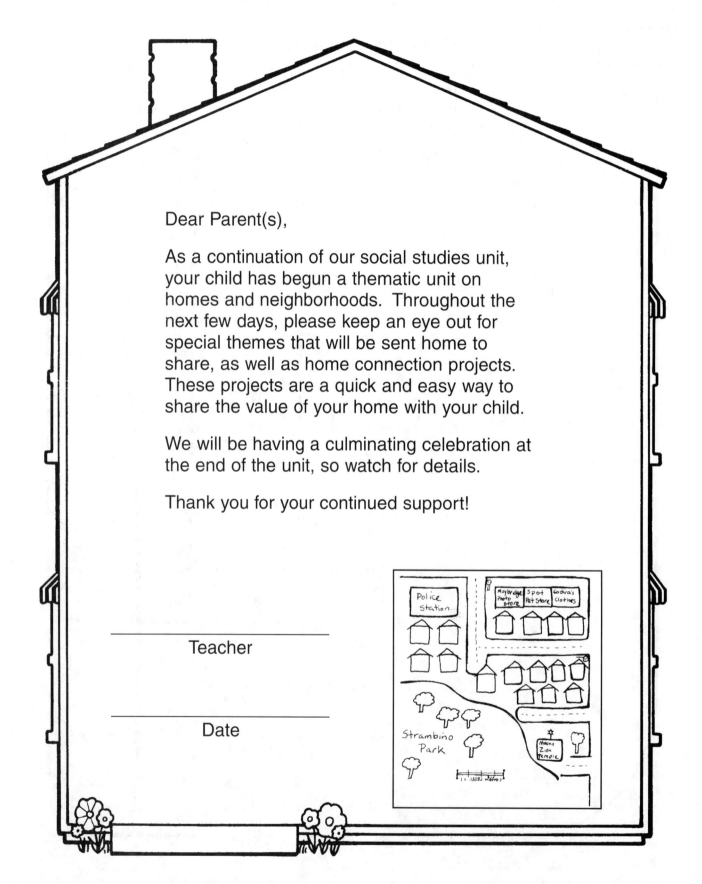

Dear Parent(s),

As a continuation of our social studies unit, your child has begun a thematic unit on homes and neighborhoods. Throughout the next few days, please keep an eye out for special themes that will be sent home to share, as well as home connection projects. These projects are a quick and easy way to share the value of your home with your child.

We will be having a culminating celebration at the end of the unit, so watch for details.

Thank you for your continued support!

_____
Teacher

_____
Date

Home in a Bag

Dear Parent(s),

As a special introduction to our unit on My Home and My Neighborhood, please help your child choose something to represent each of these categories. Please choose 3-D items that are unique and able to fit inside the attached brown bag. Some ideas are listed below. These items will be sent home with your child on_____. Be creative!

_____

Teacher

Items

- a hobby or free-time activity that I enjoy

- favorite book

- what I want to be when I grow up

- something I'm good at

- a place I'd like to visit

- summer vacation

- something of which I'm proud

Safety at Home

Dear Parent(s),

Your son or daughter has been learning about safety at home. You can further his or her learning by practicing your phone number with your child.

Once your child has memorized the number, please sign, detach, and return so that he or she may receive a special reward in class!

Thank you,

_____
Teacher

_____
Date

Homework

Dear Parent(s),

As a follow-up of today's lesson, please allow your son or daughter to help with an appropriate job around the house tonight. Please sign and return the bottom portion tomorrow.

Thank you!

Tonight,_____ helped at home. _____ doing the

following: _____

_____

_____
                Parent Signature

- -

Neighborhood Map

Dear Parent(s),

As a continuation of our learning about our neighborhoods, our class would like to make a map showing where each one of us lives. This map will be posted on the classroom wall from_____ to_____. We are working on our beginning mapping skills, so your help and cooperation are greatly appreciated!

Please sign and return this information by_____, so that no one is left out of our mapping adventure!

Please write **only the name of your street, not your house number,** on the line below. Thank you for your help!

_____   _____
        Street Name Only   Parent Signature

Home Sweet Home

Make enough copies of the following letter to send home with each student. Circle or highlight one to two items for each student to donate toward the activity. Not all items are necessary, so if it is too much for a small class to bring all items, circle only the ones you think are necessary. Other decorative goodies can be used, such as a colorful cereal. A few boxes would suffice to meet the needs of a whole class. Send the letter home with students, making sure that it is clear to them as well as to parents that only the items circled should be brought to class.

- -

Dear Parent(s),

On_____, we will be making graham-cracker houses to celebrate the completion of our "home" units. This is a big project, so the more volunteers we have, the better. A sign-up sheet will be posted on our classroom door if you are able to attend.

Please bring only the items highlighted or circled by_____. If you have any questions, please let me know!

Thank you,

_____

- two packages Red-Hots®
- two packages gumdrops
- five packages LifeSavers®
- colored candy sprinkles
- red string licorice
- pretzel sticks
- large package of M&M's®
- two boxes powdered sugar

- miniature Tootsie Rolls®
- colored mini-marshmallows
- 25 plastic knives
- 25 large paper plates
- two boxes graham crackers
- mini candy canes
- Necco wafers
- two cans meringue powder

Home Connections

The following ideas have been designed to enable students to continue learning about their homes from their families. These ideas can be sent home with the Home Connection Sharing Themes on page 68 or can be assigned through some other means if necessary.

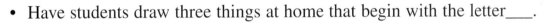

- Have each student ask a family member what he or she likes about living at home. Students should share responses the next day.

- Have students bring something from their backyards. Set parameters for the students regarding the bringing of live things from outside. It is suggested that you allow for plants to be brought in, but no animals. You'll be amazed at students' creativity. Allow time to share.

- Have students draw three things at home that begin with the letter___.

- Explain to students that they are going to go on a letter hunt. They will be detectives, so they will have to use their minds to look for clues. Choose a letter and pass out the Letter Hunt! activity on page 16; have students walk around their homes, drawing items they see that begin with that sound. This can also be done using ending sounds or common series of letters.

- Students may bring in one favorite toy to share with classmates.

- Have students conduct their own "treasure hunt" at home. Guide students toward seeing their homes as places that protect things that are important to them. Show students important things kept at your home, such as pictures, letters, etc. Allow students to bring in and to share their own treasures from home.

- Have students make a rubbing of the outside wall of their home using an unwrapped crayon. Explain to students how to put the paper over the surface of the wall and gently slide the crayon side to side to show the texture of the wall.

- Have students perform one job at home to help their parent(s) take care of their homes. Send "Homework" letter home, page 69.

- Students should bring in pictures of their homes to share with the class. Give students the opportunity to be proud of the place where they live. Let each student answer a question from an interested classmate.

- Students should go on a walk around their neighborhood with a parent or other safe adult. Ask them to count how many items they see. Students should record numbers on the Neighborhood 3–2–1 Hike worksheet on page 57.

Flannel Pieces Construction

To make flannel pieces, follow the instructions below.

1. Color the pieces.
2. Cut the pieces around the edges.
3. Laminate the pieces if desired.
4. Glue felt onto the back of each piece, just one strip large enough to hold the piece on a flannel board.

Variations:

If you do not have a flannel board, follow steps one through three, then adhere a piece of magnet to the back of each piece. They can now be used as visual aids on a magnet board or a cookie sheet.

Another option is to use Velcro strips and carpet squares. Again, follow steps one through three, then place the rough side of Velcro on the back of the piece, and display the pieces on carpet squares. For the Velcro to adhere, the carpet must not be shag. Carpet squares may be provided for free to your class if you ask a nearby carpet store to donate some old samples. Test each square to make sure that Velcro will stick.

Patterns can also be reproduced onto index paper or tagboard.

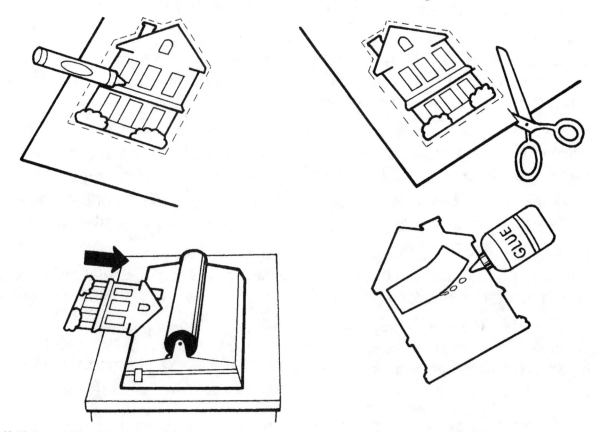

Big Book Construction

1. Tape down the left side of the back page to a tabletop.

2. Working from the back to the front of the book, add and tape down each page to the left side.

3. Lift up all pages and fold the tape edges around the left side.

4. Cover the bindings with strong, wide tape. (Try electrical or duct tape.)

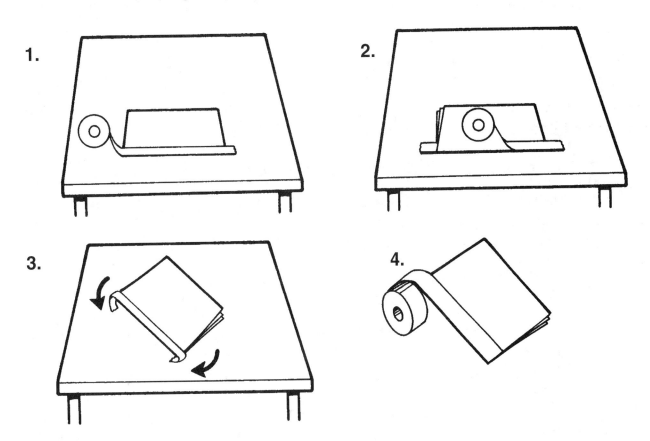

Variations:

Big books can also be bound by using a hole-punch and yarn. Simply punch three holes in each page, one at the top, one in the middle, and one at the bottom. Reinforce the holes with clear tape, punching again. Next, tie yarn through each hole, allowing room for pages to turn.

You can also bind the big book by using a spiral bought at any copy store. The store should have a spiral punch available to use. Punch each page and attach the spiral as directed by the clerk. These hold up nicely and are usually inexpensive.

Finally, books can also be bound by using clasping metal rings and a hole-punch. First, punch pages as mentioned above, and rather than using yarn, use clasping metal rings to hold pages together.

Yesterday and Today
Bulletin Board

Objectives

This bulletin board has been designed as a tool to help reinforce skills taught/reviewed. Use the Yesterday and Today Flannel Pieces on page 12 as patterns for items. These must be enlarged, colored and laminated.

Materials

butcher paper or fabric (for background), white construction paper for flannel pieces, black marker (for outlining details), markers, scissors, and staples or pushpins.

Construction

1. Reproduce pattern pieces on page 12; color, laminate, and cut out.
2. With the black marker, add details to the patterns.
3. Staple or pin background into place.
4. Add patterns.
5. Add title.

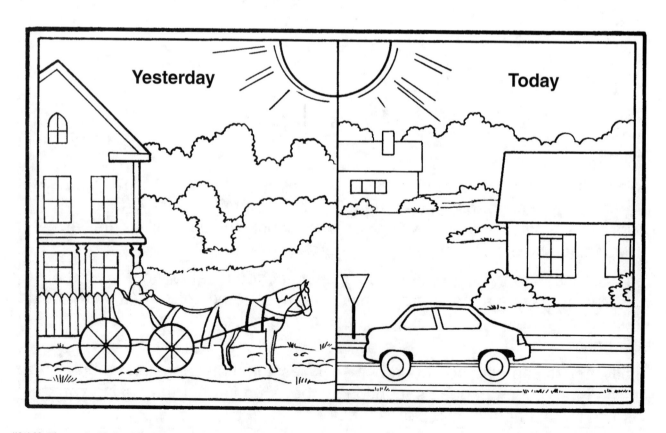

In a People House
Bulletin Board

Objectives

This bulletin board has been designed as a tool to help reinforce skills taught/reviewed, as well as to display student-made products.

Materials

butcher paper or fabric (for background), white construction paper for family portraits on page 9, black marker (for student names), scissors, hole-punch, yarn, and staple or pushpins.

Construction

1. Reproduce Family Portrait on page 9; color, and hole-punch.

2. With the black marker, add student names.

3. Staple or pin background into place.

4. Thread pictures with yarn to hang.

5. Add title.

I'm Home! Bulletin Board

Objectives

This bulletin board has been designed as a tool to help reinforce skills taught/reviewed, as well as to display student-made products.

Materials

butcher paper or fabric (for background); red butcher paper to make roof, white construction paper for student work from Setting the Stage #5 on page 6; black marker (for student names); scissors; hole-punch; and staples or pushpins.

Construction

1. Complete pictures of rooms.
2. With the black marker, add student names.
3. Staple or pin background into place.
4. Add large red triangle to make roof of home.
5. Add title.

Our Treasures from Home Bulletin Board!

Objectives

This bulletin board has been designed as a tool to help reinforce skills taught/reviewed, as well as to display student-made products.

Materials

butcher paper or fabric (for background); white construction paper for student work from Our Treasures From Home on page 34; black marker (for student names); scissors; sandpaper; and staples or pushpins.

Construction

1. Reproduce pattern piece for Treasure Chest on page 34; color, and laminate.

2. With the black marker, add student names.

3. Staple or pin background into place.

4. Add sandpaper to bottom of board to give the appearance of the ocean floor.

5. Add student work and centerpiece.

6. Add title.

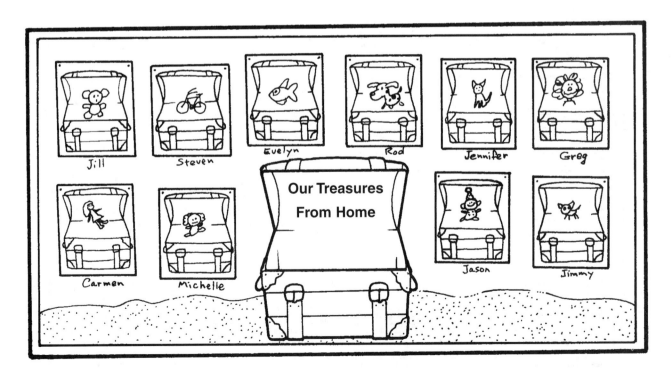

This Is Our Neighborhood Bulletin Board!

Objectives

This bulletin board has been designed as a tool to help reinforce skills taught or reviewed, as well as to display student-made products.

Materials

butcher paper or fabric (for background); Me on the Map, Extending the Book #1 and #2 on page 55; pictures taken during walk around neighborhoods, or patterns of Community Buildings from page 64; black marker (for student names/building names); scissors; black construction paper; and staples or pushpins.

Construction

1. Label each drawing/photo with community building name and student name (if drawn).

2. If using patterns from page 64, color, cut, and laminate each.

3. Staple or pin background into place. Arrange drawings, photos, or patterns around board.

4. Use black construction paper cut into three- to four-inch (7.5–10-centimeter) strips to show streets. Use street sign patterns from page 65 to post names of streets.

5. Add trees and shrubs if desired.

6. Add title.

This Is Our Neighborhood

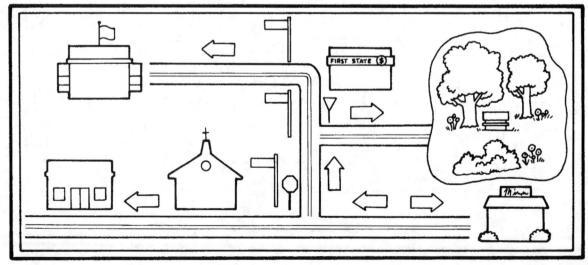

Stationery Pattern

Bibliography

Core Books

Carle, Eric. *A House for Hermit Crab.* Scholastic, 1987.

Celsi, Teresa. *The Fourth Little Pig.* Ingram Publishers, 1993.

Le Sieg, Theo. *In a People House.* Random House, 1972.

Sweeney, Joan. *Me on the Map.* Crown Publishers, Inc., 1996.

Book Nook/Supplemental Reading

Alexandria, Virginia. *Who Named My Street Magnolia?* Time Life for Children, 1995.

Anno, M. *Anno's U.S.A.* Putnam and Grosset Group, 1983.

Barton, Byron. *Building a House.* William and Morrow & Co., 1981.

Emberley, Rebecca. *My House: A Book in 2 Languages.* Little, Brown & Co., 1990.

Florian, Douglas. *A Chef.* Greenwillow Books, 1992.

Florian, Douglas. *An Auto Mechanic.* Mulberry Books, 1994.

Herman, Gail. *There Is a Town.* Random House, 1996.

Kalman, Bobbie. *A Colonial Town: Williamsburg.* Crabtree Publishing Co., 1947.

Kalman, Bobbie. *People at Work.* Crabtree Pub. Co., 1986.

Lakin, Patricia. *Aware and Alert.* Raintree Steck-Vaughn, 1995.

Lakin, Patricia. *Signs of Protest.* Raintree Steck-Vaughn, 1995.

McGeorge, Constance W. *Boomer's Big Day.* Chronicle Books, 1994.

Patrick, Denise L. *The Car Washing Street.* Tambourine Books, 1993.

Rosen, Michael. *This Is Our House.* Candlewick Pub., 1996.

Saltzberg, Barney. *Mrs. Morgan's Lawn.* Hyperion Books, 1993.

Viorst, Judith. *Alexander, Who's Not . . . Going to Move.* Antheneum Books for Young Readers, 1995.

Wood, Audrey. *The Napping House.* Harcourt Brace and Co., 1984.

CD-ROM

Simtown. Maxis Kids, 1994. (ages 6–10)

Tonka Construction. Hasbro Interactive, 1996. (ages 4 and up)